To my family:

Thank you for always believing in me.

CONTENTS

♥

Please email inquiry.fedrau@gmail.com for public speaking or other inquiries.

INTRODUCTION

♥

"YOU'RE ONLY GIVEN ONE LITTLE SPARK OF
MADNESS. YOU MUSTN'T LOSE IT."
—ROBIN WILLIAMS

G reat spirits have always encountered violent opposition from mediocre minds" (Einstein, A). Upon concluding my literary journey of this memoir, I decided to write this introduction. Now that I have poured my soul and mascara-filled tears into this in-depth recollection of modern-day trials and tribulations, I questioned how to warn others about the raw nature of what they were about to read. Would I receive criticism and consequent opposition from those who had never endured such comprehensive pain? Possibly. However, the experiences you are about to be engulfed with are what have brought me to become the extraordinarily strong and empowered woman I am today.

As I began writing this memoir, I questioned what was too personal to include for a worldwide audience. The Oxford Canadian Dictionary defines a memoir as "A historical account or biography written from personal knowledge." If I were to have removed one of my recollections from this piece of literature, I felt like my advocacy for strength, and physical and emotional well-being would have been diminished. As such, I pray that you are able to stay seated in the theatre during the emotionally distressing, tear-stealing scenes until the lights come on at the end.

Crumpled notes were found under my bed filled with disdain and consequent underpinnings of suicidal thoughts. Empty vodka bottles riddled with diminished remnants of memories from nights prior in my adolescent years were hidden under clothes. Discoloration from punching my stomach to have it descend below my ribcage was the focus of my bedroom mirror.

My recollection of events is not for the faint of heart. However, nor is it an unrealistic portrayal of the emotional and physical distress that some come face to face with. Having endured and persevered from the events you are about to read has allowed me to become an advocate for strength, positivity, and emotional and physical health. I am merely one millennial in this crazy world and am not afraid to speak up.

ELEMENTARY COMPREHENSION

♥

"YOU MISS 100% OF THE SHOTS YOU DON'T
TAKE."
—WAYNE GRETZKY

For most people breaking a leg is meant figuratively; for me it was literal. As I stare out the window from the eighth floor of my office building in downtown Saskatoon, I see the snow melting into slush. High-end executives are strolling across the concrete below as they nonchalantly step around the various puddles beginning to form. The droplets of water that cascade down the window directly in front of me are stained from dirt and nature's blemishes, reminding me of black tears filled with mascara and remnants of vodka from nights forgotten in my adolescent years.

It all started in Grade 6, unless you want to count the time I pulled down a girl's pants in Grade 1 recess lineup to humiliate her; however, I won't start there. It's funny how even in elementary school you begin to envy others. There were Brianne and all of the "cool" girls, and two boys who were nicknamed Mustard and Ketchup who somehow fit into that stereotype as well. As for me, I was always the wanderer—never in the socially repugnant group, although never in the popular group either.

Around the time that I was finally able to enter school through the "mature" side—where students in grades 5 and 6 were allowed to enter—the song "Who Let the Dogs Out?" had just become an instant one-hit wonder. Of course, the malicious intent of those dying to be popular found a way to amend the seemingly innocent song. Before you knew it, my peers altered the lyrics to be "Who let Ali's pimples out?" and sang it obnoxiously around the entire school. Thankfully, I was soon able to sing my own song in front of the entire community and was enthusiastically applauded for doing so.

A boy whom I had grown up with for most of my life decided to undertake a duet to Shania Twain for the school's talent show with me. The outcome was a roaring sound of approbation. Upon realizing my natural talent on stage and love of entertaining, my teachers decided to push me a bit further. Soon after, I became the miniature form of an enormous celebrity who had breasts that I am admittedly now quite envious of. Prior to stepping on stage, my shirt was stuffed with blown-up balloons to resemble the celebrity's more-than-ample chest and a disheveled blonde wig placed daintily on the top of my head. Whom am I talking about? Dolly Parton, of course. My elders thoroughly enjoyed the performance, although most were probably envious of my over-abundant top section. Before long, it was time for graduation from elementary school; I went home and cried for hours. I was not ready to start fresh at an entirely new school—an all-girls school—Rivier Academy.

It was the first day of school all over again. However, this time I was not in a deranged state of mind while trying to find what to wear. I stepped out of my mom's purple minivan and dragged myself sheepishly through the large wooden doors, sporting knee-high forest-green socks, a matching kilt and a button-up white shirt that seemed to stick in all of the wrong places. Again, within the first few days it was quite easy to spot the socially disturbed and those who were ready to bite into any embodiment of gossip they could descry. Remarkably, I fit in with the popular girls, albeit this lasted approximately one week before Hell struck.

I was soon sitting with girls who resembled nothing feminine, and I soon came to the unfortunate conclusion that I would rather sit alone than with them. The loneliness from being so shallow and narrow-minded sent me into a state of emotional whiplash that in turn lashed back at me. I decided to make up a friend online to pretend I wasn't lonely—so that my peers wouldn't think I was a loner. It went as far as making fake instant-messaging conversations and bragging about them to those around me. If my own ego hadn't come into play, and I hadn't attempted to change who I was to fit in, this likely could have been avoided.

I should have known that people who turned out to be that malicious would find a way to extricate the truth. My obscure labyrinth of lies quickly came undone. My classmates had found out that I did indeed, for a short period of time, create fake instant-messaging chats. I just wanted others to think I was liked. I was soon walking into classrooms only to hear the silence of a prior conversation that was daggered at myself as blank stares looked up at me. I would sit at my desk in the corner as my peers laughed together behind me and continually talked shit about me while I was clenching my fist on the corner of my desk. My insecurities quickly led my actions to become malevolent. Soon, I was igniting fights online with my classmates just to feel superior; this was an enormous mistake. As I was quick-witted and had a sharp tongue, I could easily cause distress on my classmates while hiding behind a computer. However, the minute I walked into school I would cower. I spent every single day coming to school distressed from what was about to transpire from the loathsome looks I was already receiving.

If fear wasn't enough, my largest insecurity then had to come into play: my physical appearance. It turns out that for a small period of time, I was allergic to sweat—even small amounts. From gym class, to walking around school, to feeling warm in a classroom, I would break out in full-body hives. Red welts that covered my entire body and crept up my neck onto my face were not the epitome of beauty, which made my inner beauty disappear into a spiral of resentment. I needed a break— a break from everything. Grade 8 ended and, upon being coaxed by a boy whom I knew at the time, I decided to attend one of the largest high schools in Saskatchewan. The experiences to come are what made me believe Hell really is on earth—or so I thought.

MISLED INTRODUCTIONS

> "THE MIND IS EVERYTHING. WHAT YOU THINK
> YOU BECOME."
> —BUDDHA

It was the first day of high school. Walking alone into a complex maze of faces was extraordinarily mortifying. There were the stoners, jocks, preps, nerds, goths, skanks and every clique in between. Shortly after familiarizing myself with the building's never-ending halls, it was time for the initial welcome ceremony. As the hordes of groups fled into the auditorium, I found myself sitting alone beside a girl with disheveled hair and excessive body odor. Again, I was lonely. Little did I know that would be the epitome of what was to come.

It was time for the first class of high school—the "best years of our lives." Thankfully, as I dragged myself into the gymnasium, I saw Jacklyn and a few other girls whom I knew from years prior. They welcomed me with explosive hugs and immediately my spirit was eased. Through those girls I ended up meeting Catey. She turned out to be my best friend and confidant for what lasted one mere year. Some referred to us as Mutt and Jeff; I was tall and lanky while she was short and filled with constant energy—two traits I would have died to have had at the time. Our lunch hours were spent speeding to Booster Juice in our rundown cars while blaring music out of our windows and dancing in our seats. Our afternoons were spent laughing hysterically down the hallways while collecting looks from those who thought we were obnoxious. I finally fit in. We told each other everything and I was finally able to be myself around someone. For my birthday, she even gave me a picture frame filled with a collage of memories and quotes from our unforgettable times together, even though it was just one year.

After witnessing the party scene at school, I was in dire need to get belligerently drunk as that seemed to be a common characteristic among the prevailing crowd. That was when I had decided to accompany a girl I knew, Amy, to a small party which was located in the back of a school's playground—a setting which was less-than enticing. However, the dark and musty playground was soon filled with the crowd that I was essentially begging to be a part of. Some of the students' siblings soon pulled up in trucks and began distributing the alcohol to their friends, as we were all too young to buy it. I was soon handed a mickey of Smirnoff vodka with no mix. I started chugging the liquid state of emotional death and was soon in the care of Amy and her father. The last thing I remember is waking up on her bedroom floor beside a puddle of vomit. Although I felt like death, all I wanted to do was dive into more alcohol as I felt that it led my peers to acknowledge me.

I was soon stealing money from my parents in any way I could think of to purchase more alcohol. By the time I was 16, I was able to buy my own alcohol—a trait that many of my peers soon abused. Within one month my life was starting to fall apart. I was screaming at my parents, smacking my dad across the head and began sneaking out of the basement window just to go party with the people whom I didn't even respect.

Before long, Catey's mother had heard about my malicious behaviour. She forbid her to hang out with me. This instantly broke my heart; she was the only true friend I had at that point. The relationship ended almost instantaneously. However, I pretended not to care. I acted out even more viciously, trying to prove that the seemingly shy and insecure girl was indeed not those things. As pathetic as it sounds, my closest friend soon after that was my orange, overweight cat, Teddy. He was always there to comfort me or give me a good fight as it was needed. However, as like everything else that was happening in my life, he was soon diagnosed with cancer and died on my pillow. It's amazing how God always has a way of watching out for us, however. Approximately one week before he died, a small kitten mysteriously showed up on our doorstep. Needless to say, she soon took the irreplaceable spot of Teddy. Her name was Charley. Soon after the heartbreak of losing another friend, I was right back into my malevolent ways.

Many of the students at school were continuously discussing what seemed to be an immense drunk-fest: August Long weekend at Candle Lake. Since I had come to the realization that my peers only used me to purchase alcohol for them, which at that point I didn't care, I decided to bribe my 14-year-old neighbour to sneak out of her house and drive to Candle Lake with me for that weekend. I advised her to bring a bathing suit and told her we were going to go shopping. Before long, I had stolen my mother's minivan and we were on the way to the most prodigious of events for high school teenagers. As we pulled up, it was clear that it was going to be a party. Scattered along the ditches were parked cars with boys hollering out of their windows at the girls walking past them in skimpy bikinis. Beverly Hills by Weezer was blaring out of seemingly every vehicle with their over-abundant subwoofers amplifying the bass. There were broken beer bottles everywhere and people chugging bottles of hard liqueur while running down the streets. The situation was essentially a misdemeanor in disguise and I loved it. We parked my mom's minivan and decided to join in—ripping off our clothes and strutting down the ditches in our bikinis. It took about 10 seconds before we were picked up and were in the back of a truck drinking beer with complete strangers. I felt on top of the world. However, it wasn't long until we headed home. As dusk rose, the crowds of intoxicated young adults piled into the two most popular bars at the time. Since we were both substantially underage and figured we would likely get asked for identification, we decided to drive home.

Back at school it was clear that the majority of the "popular" students were involved in sports—namely, hockey and volleyball. As such, I attended a volleyball tryout. Although I am 5'10 and thought my height may provide me with an instant advantage, I may as well have put a large rejected sign on my forehead since the list of names of those who were chosen was posted the next day without my name. Maybe it's because I was too proud to try my hardest in front of others and still get rejected, but I guess I'll never know. Subsequently, I decided to try for basketball—surprisingly succeeding. At first, I felt unbelievably jubilant that I was finally part of a group. At that point in time, all I wanted was a "bunnyhug" with my name on the back. Soon after, however, my partying took control of my mindset and I was soon skipping practices to get drunk or smoke weed—which I had done about one time up to that point. This was a shame since my coach had nicknamed me "the ringer" as I was surprisingly good at sinking the ball.

It wasn't long before I was hanging out with Amy and her friends again. She invited me to go to Shoppers Drug Mart one afternoon to go shopping; I thought it would be an innocent trip and an afternoon of hanging out with girlfriends. As we left the car and proceeded to walk into the store, she told me that none of the makeup had security tags. Therefore, she persuaded me to help her steal the untagged items—not just a tube of mascara. By the time we were ready to leave, we had our sleeves stuffed with makeup right up to our elbows. We grasped the bottoms of our sleeves with our fingers to ensure the items didn't fall out. The second we got outside, we sprinted to the car to dump the makeup in the backseat to see what we had collected: approximately $200 worth of makeup each. It seemed so easy to belligerently lie to someone's face and walk away with the products that they were supposed to protect. Of course, this escapade turned into one of many.

Another day went by and it was another Monday at school. Walking through the doors to see everyone's faces who were beginning to know my name through a misled reputation was not the welcome I looked forward to. I spent my weekends partying and becoming inebriated to escape the emotional burdens from my peers. I eventually thought that since it took away the pain on weekends, maybe it would at school as well. Getting Booster Juice with Catey at lunch hours seemed so juvenile compared to the lunch hours I was currently undertaking.

MALICIOUS INTENT

"YOUR TIME IS LIMITED, SO DON'T WASTE IT
LIVING SOMEONE ELSE'S LIFE."
—STEVE JOBS

A cross the street from school was Seven Guns Saloon: a grungy old pub, outlined in rustic wood, whose inside appearance, including the customers', was nothing to be worthy of. However, my dark hair, height and "I-don't-give-a-shit" attitude apparently led the owners to believe I was over 19 years of age—the legal age for purchasing alcohol in Saskatchewan. As soon as the lunch bell rang, I would walk over to the pub with a few of my "friends," who all along I knew were my complete antagonists. While they waited in the alley behind the pub, I would be in and out within five minutes with a few Big Bears—repulsive, cheap beer—in hand. Even the alcohol sought from the pub was not appreciable. I would walk around to the back of the pub and re-enter the friend's car. We would sit in there for a good half-hour before going back to school; however, school was a bit different this time around. Barely walking and dragging myself into school, a couple of the teachers took notice. I was noticeably drunk. It's funny how by this point they knew I was going through some sort of emotional distress, so none of them said much except nicknaming me "Bobblehead" in class—for obvious reasons, of course.

Unfortunately, my confidants at that point were not only into indulging in alcohol; marijuana was a strong selling point for them as well. Before you knew it, I was catching rides with people whom I barely knew to complete strangers' houses. Inside you would find me sitting on a couch with my eyes barely open; when they were open, they were bloodshot. I was quickly becoming a teenage alcoholic and a "stoner"—which was the adolescents' accepted term. Smoking weed from blades, bongs, joints and pipes became an outraging habit. Soon, doing one or the other wasn't enough. I was "high as a kite" and was additionally consuming enough alcohol to make me pass out. It still has not hit anywhere near rock bottom.

In elementary school and the years prior to high

school I was an "A" student—always liked by my teachers and always took pride in my work. However, by this point in time my grades had plummeted to failing marks. Skipping class to get high and drunk became a daily occurrence. The part-time job I had at Foot Locker fell to the wayside as well. Now, I was skipping class, ditching work, sneaking out, stealing, and getting high and drunk—sometimes just out of boredom.

Although the girl I truly am was temporarily lost, there was always one way to reach back into my soul. Since I was very little, I was involved in piano lessons. My piano teacher always pushed me to push myself and it worked. I was enrolled in the Royal Conservatory of Music and undertook lessons once per week. By the time I was in Grade 5 with the Royal Conservatory of Music, I had received a silver medal from completing one of their exams; the exam was essentially like a written test, but aptitude for your piano-playing ability. I had received the highest mark in Saskatchewan that year and the second-highest mark in Canada. Playing piano was a temporary escape to beauty. Anyone has the ability to press the keys and create sound; however, it is so much more than that. You need to have the ability to augment the sound of your music by a simple touch and the ability to feel the music from within as you're playing it. It was a true passion of mine, which my mother knew but I was always too ashamed to admit.

By the end of my high-school years I had completed Grade 8 with the Royal Conservatory of Music with honors, which would allow me to become a piano teacher if I so sought. However, music wasn't my only passion—my writing ability was as well. On numerous occasions, teachers would compliment me on my poetry, stories and songs that I had written in no longer than usually 20 minutes. Writing was an escape from the emotional pain that was overtaking me; I could transpose all of my animosity into an enthralling piece of literature. I was good at it too. By the end of high school, two of my poems had been published. There was one downside to my writing, however. My crumpled notes of prior writings and scribbles were usually found tossed under my bedside, which my mother would almost always end up finding. The writings were dark; hatred, anguish and disdain were the main concepts, which I would find out 11 years later had caused my mother to think I was suicidal. My heart was breaking and being plunged onto paper; I wish I knew it was silently breaking my mother's heart as well. Once the piano playing had stopped and the writing was gone, it was time for me to sing *a cappella*, although it was just a silent cry for help.

Another weekend was here. My parents wouldn't let me attend parties—they would've been insane if they did—so it was time to again sneak out. The window in the basement was a large size with latches at the bottom. It was usually covered in old cobwebs, so I would cover myself in a blanket while I climbed onto the couch and crawled out of the window. At that point I didn't even know where I was going; I just wanted out. I would wander down the street at midnight calling people to come and pick me up to bring me to a party or wherever I could get drunk and borrow some weed. One of those places ended up being far on the West side of the city— the area an innocent little girl should never be found alone at night.

I walked into the door of a rundown old house with a few people I knew to find a gathering of approximately 50 others crammed into the bungalow. Fortunately, everyone was giving; I was able to get drunk for free and was constantly being given more beer, vodka and shots than I needed. By midnight, I was passed out in the closet. There were police pounding on the front door as I woke up. I had neither returned home nor told my parents where I was going, and they had just seen the window's remnants from me sneaking out the night before. This was one occurrence of an uncountable amount for four years.

I heard the owner of the house open the front door screaming at the police and my mom shrieking saying she could see my shoes. To this day I still have no idea how she found out where I was. I was terrified. I smashed open the back door of the house and began running barefoot down the back alley of some West-side shithole. Was I really running from police? I sprinted into a neighbor's shed and quickly hid before they were able to see where I ran. It worked. The next day at school the same police officer who had come to find me the morning before confronted me; I was bestowed with a lengthy colloquy based on respect, which at that point was a trait that was not part of my vocabulary.

The struggle with alcohol continued. I was now partying on weekday nights as well. When another weekend came, I decided to go back to vodka as it gave me the most incomparable intoxication level. This time, it went further than any other. My peers at the party forced me to come home. When I did, I curled up in the fetal position inside the downstairs bathroom of my house and passed out behind the door. My parents obviously knew what had happened. It now breaks my heart knowing that my father's dad had died from alcohol abuse and I was following in his footsteps. Without hesitation, my dad bolted downstairs to come save me. I was comatose—in a state of complete unconsciousness. The bathroom door was locked and I was passed out directly behind it; if he broke the door open, he broke me. Of course, that didn't stop him. He found a way to remove the door and safely stay with me while I was essentially lifeless.

Back at school everyone now knew my name. Maliciousness took on a new form, which caused my self-esteem to hit rock bottom. My peers at school decided to nickname me "Shrek" which caught on like wildfire. Shrek was known for being big, awkward, ugly and socially unacceptable—traits that I would have done anything to discharge from my name. It got to the point where I couldn't walk from class to class without hearing "SHREK" hollered at the top of someone's lungs, sending me into a state of distress. Any party I would go to from then on, people referred to me as "Shrek." The nickname secured me a spot as a loner since no one wanted to be seen with someone who was associated with that nickname. Verbal abuse was no longer enough for the invidious adolescents; the abuse soon turned into writing. I couldn't so much as go to the bathroom without seeing my name written on walls and in bathroom stalls. Upon entering a stall I would close the door and see "ALI SARCHUK IS NASTY" or "ALI=SHREK" written, in permanent marker, across the entirety of it. It's a bit disheartening when you simply walk into a bathroom to be welcomed with your name and derogatory comments plastered everywhere for students and teachers to see. I was embarrassed to show my face anywhere I went. However, I was still able to attend parties without being kicked out or being rejected when attempting to enter them.

I ended up going to a hot-tub party at one friend's house. Everything was surprisingly great. We were blaring music, laughing in the hot tub and getting wasted, which was definitely not an unusual occurrence now. However, one of the brothers thought it would be funny to put me through Hell to make himself appear superior. He said that he was going in the house to pour me another drink. When he came out, I took a sip of the vodka and immediately thought I felt a small lump go down my throat; however, I didn't think anything of it. Within a half-hour I didn't remember a thing. My friend Carissa took me back to her place as I was covered in vomit and couldn't even hold myself up straight. Sure, how about "roofie" (a common term for drug) the girl who gets loaded and smokes pot anyway. I couldn't believe that someone would put my health in jeopardy, especially in front of an entire party. I looked like a joke.

If alcohol, weed and date-rape drugs weren't enough, ecstasy then came into play. It was one night when I decided to go party in Saskatoon. Although I wasn't of age, I was constantly scanning others' identifications and reprinting them with the correct age of 19 years—a very obvious fake form of identification, but it worked. I was partying with Mark—a boy whom I had met at Candle Lake—and a couple of his friends at the time. We decided to go to a mid-sized pub in the Sutherland area of Saskatoon. As we were sitting around a table in the back corner of the pub having a few drinks, he pulled out a few pills from his pocket. They all popped them and asked if I wanted the pill as well, which turned out to be ecstasy. I hesitantly said no as I've heard that people have died from taking the pill. They then suggested that I take half of the pill—purely peer pressure, but I gave in. Within 45 minutes I felt amazing. I had never felt that happy in what seemed to be an eternity; however, I had some kind of weird jaw-clenching going on where I would grind my teeth as I spoke. My pupils turned to black and took over the entirety of my eyes. I felt like the world was my friend and I could do whatever I wanted. It felt amazing ... until it turned into an addiction. It became so bad that when I was having a bad day or was simply bored, I would pop a pill just to turn my day around. I would hide in the basement or leave the house to ensure my parents didn't see my black, oversized pupils. Thankfully, for the first little while that I was doing ecstasy, it wasn't laced with anything. That changed badly in Grade 11.

AUGMENTED ANIMOCITY

♥

"IF YOU LOOK AT WHAT YOU HAVE IN LIFE,
YOU'LL ALWAYS HAVE MORE. IF YOU LOOK AT
WHAT YOU DON'T HAVE IN LIFE, YOU'LL NEVER
HAVE ENOUGH."
—OPRAH WINFREY

I was desperate to buy ecstasy as I needed it to get my fix. As such, I decided to resort to this boy named Michael; he was infamous all around school for having an endless supply of drugs. Later that night I was supposed to attend a close friend's party at the time— Jordan's. Before leaving for the party, I took the pill of ecstasy. It turned out to be laced with cocaine and God knows what else. The ecstasy feeling from before was not the same. I sat in my car and cried; I was scared. I went to Jordan's and threw myself on the couch as I was shaking uncontrollably. I decided to chug a mickey of vodka to try and control the bad "trip," as I thought it might just be my nerves. I was soon passed out on the corner of the couch with people asking "Who is that?" because I couldn't so much as lift my head for them to see. That was the reality shock that I desperately needed. As of that point, I didn't touch ecstasy ever again. Knowing that I became nearly addicted to an extremely dangerous drug paralyzed my conscience enough for me to get it straightened out. The risk of drug use is unquestionably not worth any reward offered.

Unfortunately, the battle with alcohol and weed only continued. I really wish that people didn't know my name by this point. It was as if their main goal was to humiliate me, to which they succeeded. It was just another weekend; another party was about to commence, this time in a small town across the river. Surprisingly, I was getting along with everyone; however, little did I know that it was because they were plotting a hoax to make me look like an imbecile. As usual, I finished the alcohol I brought and wanted more. I was mooching off everyone at the party and graciously taking whatever alcohol I could get. Eventually, one jackass took notice of this and decided to put matters into his own hands. Once he had finished his beer, he decided to urinate in it— seemingly the same colour as beer. When I came near, he pretended to twist the cap off and give me a free "beer." I was so eminently intoxicated that I did not realize the "beer" he had given to me was in fact filled with urination. When I found out that's what had been done, I wanted to disappear—forever. Thankfully, I realized what had just occurred before it went any further. Since my name was now plastered around the entire community, my peers obviously thought it would make them look superior to bully me. I couldn't attend a party or gathering without some girl now starting a fight. On countless occasions I would walk in the door of a house—or the circle around a fire at one of the "pits"— and have my hair grabbed while I was being ripped backwards into a circle. I was still timid and shy so all I did was run out the door and drive away.

On one occasion, I was simply sitting on a couch with a couple of friends. Through the corner of my eye, I could see Arianna and another girl walking up to me with an increasingly fast pace. Although I wanted to pretend I was innocent, I know she was pissed off because I had kissed her boyfriend the day prior. Although I had no idea they were dating, and of course he neglected to tell me, I still understand why she wanted to fight. As she came up to me and was standing over my head screaming profanities, I simply looked to my friend who was sitting beside me. He gave me the "go ahead" nod and with one punch I would have found myself in the middle of yet another fight. However, I was alone and scared. As I stood up and had my hair pulled backwards, I ran. They chased me all the way to my car and proceeded to kick it as I struggled to insert the key into the ignition. I was shaking. Hatred is a very strong feeling when you feel it from all angles.

I truly then had no friends. My lunch hours were spent sitting in bathroom stalls crying, hoping that no one was in there to hear me. I didn't want my peers to realize that I was lonely and hurting, so I secluded myself so that no one knew where I was.

Sneaking into bars was essentially a thing of the past since I had been doing it since I was 15. However, there was finally a local bar that opened up called "Sneakers." It was the hottest bar in the city—a dance bar with girls grinding on speakers and men standing in front of them pathetically staring. By the time I was 17, I was a regular there on weekends. Eventually, the older girls who knew my name clearly did not appreciate my presence. One Saturday night I was dancing on the speaker when a glass bottle came flying at my face. Some stranger came up to me and told me I was bleeding, which turned out to be the least of it. I had an enormous black eye with swollen cheekbones and a laceration one inch below my eyelid that required stitches. I could not show my face in any setting without being abused either emotionally or physically. The next morning I was hauled into the Principal's office at school. While being confronted by teachers, they all had one common question: Was I abused? Although they were thinking my abuse was from a boyfriend, it came from the students whom they saw on a daily basis. I was too frightened to cause more distress on my part, so I kept my mouth sealed. Humiliation now seemed to be a common theme when my name was brought up.

While I was attending yet another party on the West side of the city, I became yet again excessively inebriated. This time, my peers decided to ditch me to get me out of the situation. They told me we were all going for a walk. Within two minutes of being outside, they took off sprinting in a direction and I couldn't keep up; they disappeared. I was soon wandering around the West side of Prince Albert, eventually finding myself sitting behind a gas station crying because I was lost. All it would have taken was one phonecall to my parents and I would have gone home safely but, as usual, I was too ashamed to let them know where I was. The torment and torture of my everyday life led me into a spiral of malicious intent that I took out on my parents. Hitting my dad, screaming hurtful words such as "GO TO HELL" and "I HATE YOU" to my parents, and showing utter resentment to them was a daily occurrence, consequently breaking all of our hearts. My parents were always the most supportive, intelligent and loving parents anyone could have asked for. They were, and continue to be, two of the most selfless and utmost amazing people I have ever met. Attempting to comprehend my actions now makes me physically ill.

Thankfully, there was always one person in my life whom I could be myself around and have fun with: my little sister, Heidi. Although she is four years younger than I am, to this day I still look up to her more than she knows. She was always there for me, which was a form of relief from my everyday life. On many occasions we would find ourselves driving out to Little Red—a small recreation area across the river—in my green Ford Escort and singing obnoxiously to songs on the radio. Eventually, we decided to record our ridiculous adventures. We would place the camera on top of the dashboard, blast music and sing at the top of our lungs— all while on video. The next few hours were spent laughing hysterically at the recorded videos of ourselves. She was my best friend. Soon, the same setting I spent my afternoons laughing with Heidi in had turned to an area of resentment.

For the majority of my high school years, I had made friends with a girl named Carissa. She was one year older than I was and was rough-looking, tattooed and had an attitude that could make you shudder. Yet another weekend came and I was on the way out to Little Red; the same setting which two days earlier I spent laughing with Heidi at. Around the corner from one of the countless dirt roads in the area were ball diamonds— an infamous party spot at the time. When a couple of girls and I drove up to the party, there were approximately 200 people partying in the area. Within one minute of pulling up, Carissa was kicking my car and screaming at me through the tinted windows while the crowd began to surround us. Apparently, she was mad that I had ditched her that night, which I probably did since, at the time, I did not have any respect for a single person. As I cowered in the backseat, she was reaching through the window trying to grab my hair to rip me out of the car with the intention of kicking my ass. In the distance were roughly 200 of my peers who were cheering her on.

Brianna, a girl whom I had been hanging out with at the time, was in the front seat. I screamed at her to drive away so that my car, as well as myself, wouldn't be torn apart. She put the transmission in reverse and stepped on the gas, proceeding to hit some person behind us as she tore out of the parking lot. Apparently, the person she hit was yelling "COME BACK AND YOU'RE FUCKED UP" as we squealed away—words that I desperately wish I had heard. We parked approximately three miles away. As I was crying in the backseat with my head buried into my shaking hands, I realized we had left one of the girls we came with at the party. I let Brianna take the car back to pick her up since I felt remorseful—a colossal misjudgment. As Brianna left, I was sitting alone in some unfamiliar front yard. Within five minutes of her leaving, I heard cars squealing closer and eventually stopping right in front of the yard I was having a breakdown in. It was Carissa. As soon as she got out of the car, she came running at me, screaming that she was going to "kick my ass" and hurt me. I took off sprinting behind the house and frantically exploded into a fury of fists on the stranger's door hoping he was home. Thankfully, he was. I was able to use his phone to call my parents to come and take me home, thinking my car was fine being left out in Little Red for the night. No longer than one hour had passed when I got the text message stating "Your car is trashed."

I had no clue what to think; I was simply hoping they had the information wrong. I told my parents and they soon drove out to the site of the party. The phonecall I received from my parents was one I wish I could forget. As I picked up the phone, my mom was crying hysterically and was barely able to catch her breath. When I went out to the site to see what had happened, it felt like someone had ripped out my heart and slowly cut it into pieces. My car was destroyed. All of the windows were smashed, the top of the car was pummeled in, the body was irreplaceable and even the windshield-washer spout was torn out. The majority of attendants at the party—200 of my peers whom I proceeded to see on a daily basis—had ravaged my car that was a present from my parents. The amount of hatred that went into the destruction of my property deeply cut into my soul, as I felt like it was directed straight at me. They weren't going to get away with this that easy, however. It was going to mediation.

Back at school the entire student body was whispering as I walked by; everyone knew what had transpired the night before. Students from all cliques in the school were frantically coming up to me pleading that they had nothing to do with it, while others were saying they were the main culprits. I apprehensively walked down the hallways trying not to listen to the frantic conversations that were directed my way. Pathetically, it was nice getting all of the attention at school. The situation soon went to mediation where I had to face all of the assholes who had contributed to most of the damage. I think my mother was more outraged than I was. As we sat at the large, square table accompanied by the various assholes who had destroyed a piece of my property—and my heart—I could feel my mother's anger before she even spoke. She was relentlessly protective of her baby girl.

A few weeks later, I had realized that my menstrual cycle was late. Although I've skipped over the part of meeting my first love and having my heart broken into pieces down a dirt road just past Candle Lake, this situation transpired a mere two weeks after he broke my heart. Thinking nothing of it, I went on sulking from the heartbreak I was undergoing. A couple of weeks later, there was still nothing. As I got in my car, I drove to the medical walk-in clinic in the Cornerstone area of Prince Albert. I could barely lift my feet to drag myself in there as I was shaking so frantically. As the medical assistant asked what I needed to see the doctor for, I whispered "pregnancy test." As she gave me the cup, I tried to hide it under my arm as I sheepishly crawled past the others in the waiting room to enter the bathroom. It was easier than I thought; you just pee into a cup and wait for the results. As I sat on the bed with my hands holding my throbbing head, all I could think of was holding back my tears so that the doctor would not see me breaking down. It happened anyway.

It was a matter of mere seconds until my broken heart would literally shatter on the tiled floor. As the doctor walked through the door, she looked at me with a large smile as she hesitantly said "congratulations!" I burst into tears. I looked up at her with bloodshot, swollen eyes; I was alone. I was—or at least I felt like at the time—the epitome of an adolescent mess. I was barely 18 years old and pregnant. As soon as I collected myself together—which was essentially just gathering the strength to walk out of the clinic—I sat in the driver's seat of my car and bawled. Although I hadn't spoken to my ex-boyfriend since he broke my heart down a country backroad a few weeks prior, I had to let him know what had happened and, more importantly, what was about to come. As I slammed my fists into the steering wheel and proceeded to wipe the endless tears that were flowing down my cheeks, I picked up my cellphone to call him. His brother answered. It was immediately clear that he did not want to talk to me; however, it did not take long before I whispered "I'm pregnant, but I'm getting an abortion." "Oh, okay," he replied.

Two girls whom I had known through high school but rarely hung out with immediately came over when I told them what had just occurred. One of them, Sierra, previously had a child as well within the year. As they were comforting me and trying to calm my nerves, which were at the highest peak possible, I told them I wanted an abortion. Immediately, both of them went silent. They were strongly against it and began to tell me all of the positive attributes of having a child. Within the next couple of days, I went to see my family doctor. I told her what had happened and, thankfully, she set everything up for me.

I was soon sneaking off to Saskatoon without my parents knowing. Ultrasounds, check-ups and visiting pregnancy clinics was a regular occurrence. Although I was dying for my mother to know what was going on, I was far too ashamed to tell her. However, with her intuition, it was not long before she found out what was about to happen: I was getting an abortion. When the day came, I was sitting in the waiting room, waiting for the procedure—which some said would make me regret my life. It was the best decision I had made up to that point. I was nowhere near ready to support a child, and when someone looked down upon my decision I instantly loathed them. It wasn't as if this had been a careless mistake either; I had been consistently using birth control but, as all else, it seemed like these negative experiences were bound to find me.

Before you knew it I was laying on the medical table, counting down from 10 and then I was asleep. When I woke up, everything was done. Thank God. The only downfall was that I had to use disturbingly large menstrual-cycle pads for the next while which essentially resembled diapers. My mom knew what had happened and met me in Saskatoon before the procedure was complete. Instead of being ashamed of me, she comforted me. Her words saved my life.

While I understand that there will be criticism surrounding this chapter in my memoir, my book would not be complete without it. No matter how you view this situation, it contributed to getting me to where I am today: a very strong and proud place. The reason I chose to include this very personal and emotional experience in my book is so that others—and even those who continue to be judgmental—are able to have a glimpse into the realities that some adolescents are forced to endure. I have nothing to be ashamed of and strongly believe that my memoir would not be complete without this inclusion. Do I want to have children one day? Absolutely and unquestionably. This was one choice I had to make at a very painful time in my life.

Subsequently, as everything else had went in high school, gossip soon engulfed the hallways which I walked. The entire school knew I had an abortion within two days of the procedure. Unfortunately, to my dismay, this entire ordeal had transpired approximately one month prior to my Grade 12 graduation.

My original escort to graduation was my ex-boyfriend which, like everything else, ended up not panning out. He agreed to be my escort up until one month before the ceremony and then proceeded to leave me stranded and alone, shortly after the above scenario had just taken place. Frantically panicking that I was going to be walking down the aisle alone in front of all of my classmates from high school, I was willing to take anyone as an escort. Thankfully, a couple of weeks before graduation, I found Jordan. I had hung out with him a fair amount throughout the years and he agreed to escort me. Since I was going to be walking down the aisle in front of every single person who had put me through Hell, I did not want to be seen as "Shrek" anymore. The graduation dress I had picked out was impeccable: a halter-top, tight-fitting dress with a low-cut centre, black shimmer with silver sparkles and an open back. You had to be slim to wear this dress. By the time the dress fitting came around, I had lost 15 pounds and toned up a fair amount. The dress was stunning—as was I. Although I was unbelievably excited to unveil the "new" me and reveal myself in this unbelievably sexy dress, my musical abilities were soon taken notice of as well. I was asked to play the Canadian National Anthem during the opening ceremony for graduation in front of everyone. **Everyone**. However, that required me to walk alone to the middle of a stage in front of every single one of my peers—and their friends—who were previously mentioned in this memoir.

It was finally the day of graduation. Wearing my cap and gown, I proceeded to the piano which was placed in front of the entire audience. As I dreaded the part of the speaker announcing my name—thinking that I was going to hear a deafening applause of silence—I felt the most heart-wrenching emotions of all. "Everyone please welcome Ali Sarchuk" rang over the speakers. Before the speaker was finished saying my name, the entire audience roared with applause and approbation. Trying to hold back tears, I began to play the National Anthem as the entire audience sang along. After the morning passed, it was time for the Grand March—the portion of the day where the graduates and their escorts march down the aisle in their dresses and suits in front of everyone. When it was time for us to march down the aisle, the lights came on and they announced my name. I began to walk as the lights reflected off of my shimmering, tight dress. Many were stunned by what I was wearing and the way I looked. My curled, blonde hair and slim body sent silence throughout my high school peers. I felt gorgeous, and I looked it as well. I then felt the most relieving emotions of all: high school was over.

GRADUAL ENLIGHTENMENT

♥

"IT DOES NOT MATTER HOW SLOWLY YOU GO
AS LONG AS YOU DO NOT STOP."
—CONFUCIUS

F or that summer I was blatantly unsure of what direction I was wishing to steer myself in, so I decided to relax and start fresh in the fall. Summer season was the home of a well-known country music festival—a large drunk-fest in the heart of a small town in Saskatchewan. Thousands of people pack themselves into this small town for one weekend. The setting is not short of painted trailers, homemade shirts, scantily glad girls, costumes and mud fights. It was the young adult's Heaven. I decided to attend my first year and went with a few people whom I weren't that familiar with. Needless to say, by the end of the first day I was wandering alone aimlessly, except this time I was having the time of my life. You couldn't walk down a street without people hollering at you to partake in beer darts or one of the countless drinking games found in the corners of every campsite. Everyone was friendly and around the campgrounds there were endless sounds of laughter.

Although the weekend was, so far, perfect, it was not without its mishaps. By the end of Saturday night, I had broken my ankle. How? No idea. I spent the rest of the weekend walking around on it without a care in the world. Although it was swollen to the size of a turnip, my main concern was consuming as much alcohol as possible. When I finally arrived home to my parents, I entered through the door on crutches with a cast and a sarcastic smirk on my face. With just my luck, there was an article published in the Prince Albert Daily Herald that Monday morning. The summation of events was that some girl from Prince Albert had been hit by a firetruck and broke her ankle. Apparently, she was so belligerently drunk that she did not realize she had broken her ankle until the next morning. My mother was beyond convinced that the infamous girl from the article was indeed me. It most definitely was NOT; I would have remembered being smoked by a firetruck.

Throughout my high school years, I had

dislocated my knees many, many times. Finally, some short while after entering the University of Saskatchewan in 2007, I dislocated it again. This time it was done impeccably. Up to this time, I had seen the doctor for my knees ump-teen times and it was obvious he was a bit fed up. What was my welcome back? A cast up to my crotch in a translucent pink shade. I was distraught with the doctor. The cast lasted about three weeks before I decided to take matters into my own hands. With a pair of scissors and a steak knife, I slowly sawed the cast off of my own leg—not an easy task. About halfway through the process I was worried that I had cut myself with the steak knife that was sawing through the plaster in a demented manner. Thankfully, there were no lacerations and the cast came off—albeit unsafely, but in a timely manner.

The year later my family and I were planning to go to British Columbia for my cousin's wedding. I found the perfect black dress to wear and was beyond excited to do so. There was only one problem: it didn't fit. When I decided to weigh myself on the scale—a few months prior this was a daily ordeal—I realized that I had ballooned to XXX pounds. I've decided not to state my actual weight so that I don't negatively trigger anyone in the upcoming sections of this book. If people were calling me Shrek before, what were they going to call me now? My self-esteem plummeted. Nothing fit and, if it did, you could see my rolls through the creases. Thankfully, my family was always there to give me support and tell me how beautiful I was. The support truly helped, although I was always too stubborn to admit so.

After all of the Hellish ordeals that I had undergone, I decided that my possible solution for everything was to get out of Prince Albert and move to Saskatoon. It turned out to be the best decision I had ever made, eventually. Within one month of moving to the "big city," my life had changed immensely. My respect for myself and my parents took on an entirely new meaning. My mother was finally my best friend again and I was hers as well. I finally decided to set a career for myself and entered a local college in the legal field. Of course, the time spent there wasn't without getting myself in trouble with the officials and skipping over a month's worth of classes—because they were far too unchallenging for myself—but I ended up finishing college and graduated with two diplomas with honours. Upon completion of the first course, one tragic incident took place which in turn brought myself and my father much closer.

My grandmother—his mom—was diagnosed with dementia. One day during school I found out that she had no longer than one day to live. Grandma was always feisty; she was not scared to stand up for herself and speak her mind. When I went into the care home to see her, she was limp and lifeless. She couldn't speak, couldn't move and could barely show signs of recognition. It was a miracle in disguise since my dad's family who was quite separated at that point had come together. It wasn't long before she passed away. I sat in the room watching my dad run his fingers through her thin, frail her. Before long, she was whisked away into God's hands. My dad ran into the hallway and burst into tears. Watching my grandmother die in his presence was the hardest thing I've ever had to do. However, I ran into the hallway immediately after him and gave him a very supportive hug. I loved him so much and needed him to know.

This is the point where I decided to truly make a change. I had moved to a new city, successfully completed post-secondary education and was able to start a new chapter. That's when I met Kyle who, five years later, would become my husband. Within a few months of meeting him, I had lost 40 pounds and plummeted from a size 12 to a size 6. This is when I began to feel noticed. Fast-forward a few years and I had modeled for various photographers across the province, and had promotionally modelled for local stores, restaurants, radio stations and even Budweiser. My life finally began to feel like mine.

SASHES AND STEREOTYPES

"EVERYTHING YOU'VE EVER WANTED IS ON THE
OTHER SIDE OF FEAR."
—GEORGE ADDAIR

The previous sentence in this book was written nearly eight years ago. Fast-forward to the present and you'll find a "fast-working, technologically literate, detail-oriented professional with exceptional communications skills" (Fedrau, A. *Resume*). Now, let's cut the corporate shit and get back to my everyday life.

"Our deepest fear is not that we are inadequate. Our deepest fear is that we are powerful beyond measure" (Williamson, M). When I began writing this memoir nearly eight years ago, I simply wanted to portray the trials and tribulations that were found in one adolescent's life: mine. I wanted those who were to read my heart-drenched literature to know that they are not alone, thereby hopefully finding comfort in knowing that others were there with them as well. However, as I enter the last year of my twenties, I now, more than ever, want to tear my heart out of my chest and throw it on this paper in hopes of bringing some bright, vibrant colour to anyone who needs it.

Eight years ago I thought that I could never encounter further pain than I had during my high school years. Now, at the end of my twenties, I'm able to reflect on competing as a national competitor in Miss Universe Canada, overcoming stereotypes and beating a debilitating eating disorder.

Coming out of my adolescent years with the pain of being called "ugly" and "Shrek" without question caused animosity towards those who were able to hurt me for so long. If I were to say I didn't want to yell "fuck you" and prove them wrong I would have been flat-out lying. As such, I applied for Miss Universe Canada and was accepted as the only national competitor from Saskatchewan in 2012. Although this was unquestionably one of the best weeks of my life—the best being my wedding in Jamaica—this was only a precursor for a nearly eight-year-long battle with an eating disorder.

I don't quite remember how the application process went; however, it was late in 2011 when I decided to hit "submit" on my application to compete in one of the most prestigious beauty pageants in existence.

One girl whom I had grown up with in Prince Albert had competed in a less-reputable, yet still renowned pageant a couple of years prior. Although she was one of the ones who continuously attempted to put me through distress, essentially since I was two years old, her actions were easy to push to the background. She was unquestionably one of the most disliked girls in the city at the time, albeit nothing much has changed. My acceptance to compete in this pageant must have angered her. One night while my sister was out dancing at a local bar in Saskatoon, she confronted her in the women's bathroom as she scoffed "Your sister is kind of weird, hey?" Rule number one: If you fuck with me, you have a problem with my sister. That one statement was enough to solidify my sister's hatred for her as well. However, looking back at the situation, it's easy to see that we're now in an age where social media further extends the jealousy that some feel. I'm sure that seeing my face on television and in various newspapers was joyous to her, so I wasn't too upset after hearing what had occurred since it was clear to me that her insecurities had taken over.

Although I don't remember specifics, submitting pictures, an autobiography and affirmation that I was a "naturally born female," as I recall, were all found within the application. A short while later and I had received the email stating that I was accepted as the only Saskatchewan competitor to compete in Toronto in May of 2012; the winner would compete in Las Vegas on the international Miss Universe stage later that year.

Before I jump into details about the weeklong adventure of five-inch heels, hair extensions and Toronto-born bitches, I'll bring you back to a few months prior. In January of 2012 my then-boyfriend— now husband—and I were off to Jamaica for a week on the beach. Having dislocated my knees countless times in previous years and being a self-designated klutz, one would assume that sports, of any kind, should be out of the question, especially with Miss Universe Canada looming on the horizon. However, the very first morning in Jamaica I had turned the next few months of my life sideways.

Although I am a self-designated klutz, I do still enjoy competing in non-contact sports. When Kyle and I woke up the first morning in Jamaica, it began as any other. We grabbed a bit of breakfast, some kind of tropical drink—albeit it was likely 9 a.m.—and a basketball. As I was designated the "ringer" in high school for being able to sink the ball more often than not, I—of course—had to brag about this directly to Kyle's face. Thus, we began playing "21"—a game of sinking 21 balls first—at roughly 9 a.m. It must have only been a few minutes before I was laying on the ground with an audience surrounding my immediate line of sight.

I don't recall how many balls I had sank up this point; however, it was Kyle's turn to throw. He arched his arms, the ball went up and he missed. As it rolled down the pile of rocks in the distance, my uber-competitive, egocentric self—at that time—was sprinting after the ball to prove that I could win. Within a couple of steps down the rocks followed by a painful landing, I would later be told that I had torn the ligaments in my ankle—an injury that is commonly found more painful than a fracture. As I laid on the concrete in tears, the audience around me became larger and larger with every ticking second. It was only a few moments before I had been lifted onto a wheelchair for an initial assessment by the resort's staff. It was a very quick realization that I required further inspection; as such, the taxi was called and Kyle and I were on our way to one of the local Jamaican hospitals.

As the taxi van pulled up, I essentially threw myself onto the back seat as Kyle climbed in after me. My ankle felt like a hot washcloth thrown over a beating heart that was slowly being torn in half. It hurt like a bitch. Now, although I don't smoke, I must have gone through at least a couple packages of cigarettes during that short taxi ride. My trucker mouth turned into an old, beat-up Ford that was hitting potholes every second. I was smoking like crazy and screaming profanities to try and exhale the physical pain and emotional distress that were taking over my mind. As we pulled up to the hospital, the staff once again seated me on a wheelchair and pushed me into one of the waiting rooms. As I was only dressed in a string bikini at this point, the nurse had covered my bottoms with a towel and handed me a robe. As she did so, she turned my wheelchair and quite literally rammed my ankle into the side of the bed. I wanted to punch her in the face.

Now, nearly everyone—and most certainly my husband and I—know that travel insurance is an unquestionable purchase when travelling on vacation. This situation was no different; we had purchased travel insurance prior to leaving. Upon a quick examination by the Jamaican doctor, he advised that I would need x-rays, antibiotics and crutches just to start. As we gave him the contact information for our insurance, he was on the telephone with our insurance representative for quite a while. The insurance company continually advised that they had faxed over the proof of insurance, which the doctor—quite questionably—never received. As we were financially instable at the time, we were not able to pay for what needed to be done. As such, a couple of choice words and a pair of crutches later, we stormed out of the hospital and were headed back to the resort. I'll fast-forward through the countless joints—not those found in the body—and a week of exploring Jamaica in a wheelchair to get you back to the pageant.

Upon being accepted into Miss Universe Canada, one of the requirements was to secure sponsors to pay for not only your entrance fee—that consisted of flights, hotels and meals—but also to assist with pre-pageant preparations such as aesthetics, fashion and the ball gown. In the midst of securing my sponsors is when the media began to blow-up. The Miss Universe organization—at that time—was owned by Donald Trump. One of the rules which I thought I had seen clearly stated in the application process was that the applicant must be a naturally born female. As it turns out, one of the accepted competitors was indeed born a man and, when challenged by Trump to withdraw from the pageant, fired back at him with the assistance of one of the most sought-after attorneys in North America: Gloria Allred. To provide a quick summation, Trump's rule was reversed and she was indeed allowed to compete. Whether or not I agreed with this at the time can be a story for another day.

Immediately prior to leaving for Toronto, my afternoons were filled with endless physiotherapy appointments to try and get my ankle able-enough to strut in five-inch heels. Amidst warnings of further injuring my ankle from pushing it too hard, my bags were packed and I was off to the airport to compete in one of the most reputable pageants in the world. Now, I have to share what my parents arrived to the airport in for my send-off: a pair of matching t-shirts that read in large pink letters "Go Ali – Miss Universe Canada." I felt as good as freshly baked cookies taste on Christmas morning.

Upon arrival in Toronto it was an instant whirlwind of hairspray, judgement and women— countless amounts of women. As I am a bit of an introvert by nature, I grabbed my sash which read "ALI" in large red letters and sat in a chair in the corner as I waited for my turn in the makeup artist's chair. Within a couple of minutes, my soon-to-be roommate for the week had found me and introduced herself. Although her personality was a bit Chihuahua-based—quirky, high-pitched and overly exuberant—she seemed to be kind and friendly. Within the first few hours of my Toronto arrival, my hair and makeup were done, we were handed our bikinis and five-inch heels of death, and were off to partake in our first photoshoot.

Upon putting on the bikini, I immediately realized that the stereotype surrounding plastic surgery in pageants was, for the most part, accurate. For natural-chested women such as I, the top of the bikini seemed to frown rather than have the large spherical-shaped features that those who had bought were flaunting. There were girls patting their stomachs chanting "tiny tummies club" and various cliques beginning to form—namely, one Russian-speaking Toronto-based clique that tried to talk shit behind everyone's back in Russian until, that is, one girl outside of the clique could understand what they were saying. After the first approximately 19-hour working day was done, I crashed. Day one was done.

The majority of the week was now spent with 18-hour days filled with countless hours of choreography— while my ankle was tightly bandaged and I was barefoot barely able to walk—or in one of our various appearances around Toronto. My dancing experience up to this point had been fairly limited; it consisted of recitals in my younger years where I would accidentally kick my sandals off into the crowd or sloppily dancing in bars with my girlfriends. Although I was well aware that my technique—or lack thereof—was not up to par with that of the Canadian Football League cheerleaders' and dance instructors' who surrounded me, I wanted to be at the front of the stage. Consequently, I gave the auditions during the choreography lessons my all. As we began to learn the choreography and dance in rows, a couple of the instructors would narrow down the girls one by one. They would choose who would perform at the front of the stage, with altered choreography from those who were chosen to perform at the back. Everyone had been chosen except for myself and a couple of other girls who continued to perform the choreographed steps. Finally, they simply sent us all to the back. While I could easily learn the choreography, I am just a frickin' awkward dancer. Maybe it's the fact that I walk like a baby giraffe, but I had to be honest with myself and know that I saw that coming.

One of the appearances around Toronto to this day still engulfs my mind when reminiscing on this week. As the 62 women piled onto the bus for another day of appearances, we were driven to a small Catholic school with the opportunity to speak to the students about bullying. As we were not previously aware that we may be speaking, the pageant co-ordinator began to select girls to speak as we were on the bus ride to the school. My published autobiography on the Miss Universe Canada website was an open book into my heart. I unveiled my struggles with bullying and the correlating success that I had achieved after. I was and am, to this day, a strong advocate for eliminating bullying and wanted so badly to be called. Approximately 10 girls ended up being called to speak, the majority of whom had no relation to these real-life events which engulfed my adolescent years. As I pulled my short, flowy skirt down as far as I could upon the realization we would be speaking to a young Catholic school, I waited patiently as I stared out of the bus window. With every name called, I attempted to make eye contact with the co-ordinator to grasp some sort of connection.

Although I was not chosen to speak, one competitor—the winner that year—walked up to the front of the audience as she was called. The click of her heels came to a stop as she stood front and centre in front of the hundreds of children and teachers in the gymnasium. She chugged the water bottle that she was holding and immediately proceeded to crush it as forcefully as possible onto the ground. The water bottle was crumpled and cracked. She referred to herself as the bottle when she was being bullied. It was such an empowering, insightful and knowledgeable speech that I was slightly relieved that I did not have to speak following her. Upon return to the hotel, she came up to me and told me how impressed she was with my written autobiography and how much she related. In that moment—aside from being somewhat star struck—I also felt not alone.

One of the conversations I had prior to leaving for Toronto was with one of my coworkers at the time. At that point I remember saying "I don't care if I win, it's a free trip to Toronto." Although I said it, it was absolute bullshit. The pain and insecurities that burdened me from previous years were what I desperately wanted to be hidden when competing. I applied for the pageant because I wanted to be seen as beautiful and become a public advocate for mental and physical health; however, I was terrified of losing.

It was nearing the end of the week and by this point my ankle, if the bandage was off, had tripled in size. I would need to compress the ankle with my bandage for hours prior to walking in heels just to be able to fit it in the ankle strap. While we were out for dinner at the Trump Tower Hotel—which had a beautiful, gothic-themed ambiance—I had asked one of the pageant co-ordinators if I was able to wear flat shoes for the final pageant, essentially for my safety. The only reason I had asked was because I had seen numerous women with injuries do so on the international stage and even place within the top 10. I barely finished getting the last word of the question out of my mouth before a resounding "no" was hollered back at me. "If you can't wear heels then you can't walk on the stage," she scoffed. I was disgusted.

The final night was now here. The preliminary competition was the night prior, and we were about to be live-streamed to the entire world with my own family sitting in the audience. I didn't want to let them down yet again. As all 62 of us were not-so-patiently waiting backstage for the announcer to come over the speaker, I was yanking the back of my red, flowy dress down as much as possible to show off the open back. This may have just been a fidgeting strategy, however, as the rest of the time was spent anxiously reviewing each step to the choreography that we were about to flaunt on stage.

I'll be honest, I also didn't want anyone to know that while I was dancing on the top step of the stairs which were front and centre on stage, I was mainly trying not to fall off.

The evening began with the opening dance routine. I struggled my way through that but it was successful. Then it came time for the announcement of each competitor's name with their walk across the stage. I was terrified. This was the moment that allowed my insecurities to flourish. If I failed, would I look like a joke? The entire week was spent gallivanting around Toronto feeling the most beautiful I had felt in my life. I no longer needed appreciation from those with bigoted minds to have self-confidence and know I was indeed not those hurtful things I was previously called. But, what if I failed?

It must have been mere seconds before my name was called. Because of the extraordinary adrenaline that was pumping throughout my body, I instantly felt no pain. I took a couple of steps backstage just to reaffirm my mind, and I again felt no pain. Then, the speaker announced "Ali Sarchuk." My heart dropped and I took my first step onto the large stage with the spotlight directly upon me. I began to walk as the spotlight shone directly down on me in my light-pink, sequin-filled floor-length gown as I whipped my long platinum blonde hair around a little. It was done. The walk was done. Whether or not I felt pain—either physically or emotionally—I felt beautiful. Then came the announcement of the top 20.

As all 62 women were standing on stage desperately waiting for their names to be called, each chosen competitor walked up to the front of the stage one by one. The top 20 were narrowed down to the top 12, which were then narrowed down to the fourth runner up all the way to the first runner up and, eventually, the winner. With the announcement of every name it felt like a dagger into my heart. I was standing on stage, perfectly posed, waiting for my name to be called. Again, what if I failed? The smile that I had to preserve in front of the entire world was diminishing with every announcement. Then came the realization that I was not chosen. The top 20 women all competed for the chance to be crowned Miss Universe Canada 2012 while I again fell into the background and walked with the 42 others off stage.

The pageant was done. The week was done. I had made the front page of my local newspaper, completed numerous media interviews, and had received appreciation and apology messages from those who had put me through Hell in high school. Were they kissing my ass? Absolutely, but it felt great. As I walked out the doors of the Arts Centre to meet my mom, dad, sister and now-husband, there was not one mention of failure. They were so proud of me and, although I was horrifically upset and embarrassed by the outcome, I could not have been happier that they were there for support. Although the pageant was full of stereotypical attributes, it was one of the best yet most-challenging weeks of my life.

Although my pageant journey took place in 2012, it was early in 2018 when another pageant organization chose to amend its structure to remove the controversial bikini portion of the pageant. Of course, having competed in a bikini competition during a pageant, I had to weigh in on this amendment.

There are, and will forever be, stereotypes that surround pageants. Were some of those proven to myself when I competed in Toronto? Absolutely. However, I was also introduced to some of the most intelligent and confident women I have ever met who, indeed, happen to be externally beautiful as well.

For me, the bikini competition is a tradition among the various pageants. There will forever be those who think pageants are ridiculous; that will never change. Are contestants subjecting themselves to scrutiny based upon their appearances? Unquestionably.

However, there is so much more than what bigoted minds restrict themselves to seeing.

Based on my experience, I had met lawyers, nurses, valedictorians and countless others who were among the most intelligent, confident and beautiful women I have ever met. The bikini competition is no secret; every single applicant and competitor was well aware that they were indeed required to walk across a stage in a bikini. For me, it gave me a goal to achieve physically. I thoroughly enjoyed pushing my physical limits so that I was confident walking across the stage in my white, scrunched-butt bikini, even though the top could have used some extra "oompf" below it.

The stigma will always be there. Pageants will always be associated with physical beauty. However, physical beauty is only a complement to the underpinnings of what a contestant brings to the stage. Although I am in favour of the bikini competition, I strongly believe that there has to be further education within society. Just because an individual is seen as fit, she may have just thrown up her last meal. Alternatively, just because an individual has a few extra pounds, they may very well be able to out-lift and out-run the seemingly fit competitor standing next to them. Society, as a whole, needs to be open-minded and be far more aware of the societal issues present today. My week as a contestant in Miss Universe Canada, including the bikini competition, was one of the most empowering, challenging and enjoyable weeks of my life.

OBSCURE DESTRUCTION

♥

"TWO ROADS DIVERGED IN A WOOD, AND I – I
TOOK THE ONE LESS TRAVELLED BY, AND THAT
HAS MADE ALL THE DIFFERENCE."
—ROBERT FROST

As I begin to write one of the final chapters to my book, I am instantly overcome with anxiety. I want to accurately depict the emotional pain endured from suffering from a nearly eight-year-long battle with an eating disorder; however, I do not want to come across suicidal. I am struggling with the want to throw my previous anguish onto this paper, but—in all honesty—do not want to scare my family or give them guilt from not knowing just how bad this was.

As previously mentioned, competing in Miss Universe Canada was a pre-cursor for a nearly eight-year-long battle with an eating disorder. However, as I now reflect back, I think I may have been mistaken. From having my physical appearance excruciatingly and publicly criticized for so long during my adolescence, I believe that's where it truly began. When you hear that you're fat, look like a man, resemble Shrek or are simply "a mess," you want to hide ...or change. Now, let's fast-forward through my 40-pound weight loss and Miss Universe Canada, and jump to my arrival home from Toronto.

Upon my arrival home, one of the first things I did was weigh myself. I stepped on the scale, anxiously awaited the calculation and was presently surprised when XXX.X pounds flashed before me, especially since the pageant co-ordinators thought it was appropriate to continually feed us pizza throughout the week. The morning of my departure to Toronto, I had weighed in at the lowest weight of my adult life. This is when my obsession with weight began.

Having endured such negativity throughout high school, it felt so good to have people—everyone—comment on how good I looked—now that I had lost weight. Cue my obsession. Up to this point, the lowest weight I had reached was XXX.X pounds. What was the lowest weight I could hit? How quickly could I hit it? Every day now became a journey to reach the lowest weight possible. The average recommended caloric intake for basic survival for a woman—which is still very low—is based around 1,200 calories. I quickly made my daily caloric intake no more than 500 calories per day which is right where my eating disorder truly began.

My full day of eating was easy to figure out at the beginning: one Greek yogurt cup for breakfast, nothing until supper, and a medium-sized supper to reach no more than 500 calories per day. The scale dropped and dropped, and my mindset was consequently completely, excuse my blatant language, fucked. Now, many people think it would be impossible to function off of this lack of calorie consumption; however, when I was eating "perfectly" (i.e., 500 calories per day), I felt on top of the world. I had endless amounts of energy, at the beginning, because I felt like I was achieving success. Nothing tastes better than skinny feels, right? I hope you sense my severe sarcasm.

When you're consuming such few calories per day, this eventually does begin to wear on you. Although the scale did keep dropping, I was becoming emotionally and physically fatigued. Wanting to not "mess up" by eating one "bad" meal began to now engulf my every thought. I would sleep in until 12 p.m. just to try and mask the hunger I felt every single minute of every day. The stress from trying to live off of 500 calories per day also began to give me headaches, but I couldn't take any form of medication to assist. Would popping an Advil or Tylenol put extra calories into my body? Give me a fucking break. However, this is now where my mindset was at. If I were to consume even just one pill, that was unwanted "calories" and my day would be a consequent failure. As such, I tried to sleep away the pain as much as possible.

Undertaking everyday tasks soon became exhaustive. On top of limiting myself to 500 calories per day, I was also doing approximately one hour of cardio per day just to get rid of as much fat as possible. I was exhausted. I was not allowing myself the calories needed to have energy to get through the day, and was spending countless hours on the elliptical and treadmill with no fuel. This is when any friendships that I had at the time began to suffer.

Friends and family would invite me to countless gatherings and I began to say no every single time. Not only was I saying no because I was just physically exhausted from essentially starving myself, but now the anxiety of having to eat perfect on any given day completely took over my mind. If I were to attend a barbecue or movie, there would be temptations. I could not allow myself anything outside of my "meal plan" or I would fail. My best friend at the time would simply ask to hang out at her place and I would say no. If I went there hungry, I would have to struggle with the stress of fighting temptations the whole time. Did I want to spend time with my friends and family? Of course. However, my mind was now telling me that I had to eat "perfect" which, at that point, meant next to nothing.

Although I was comprehensively exhausted by this point, all I had to do was suck in my stomach to the point where I couldn't breathe and look in the mirror. As I looked in the mirror, I could see my ribs protruding about four inches out over my stomach, with each rib clearly visible as I twisted and turned. The bottom portion of my stomach fell below my hipbones, and when I was angry or upset I would "suck in" and feel my hipbones to make me feel happy again. This obsession is very, very dangerous and is also what needs to be eliminated from the exploding social media scene. Although I was in the midst of my eating disorder, I was never afraid to share my story when others were feeling down.

During one party we were hosting, one of my sister's friends came up to me and questioned how I stayed so lean. I essentially had verbal diarrhea as I stated that I struggled and would continually punch my stomach or put weights on it as I was laying down to try to suck it in. I said it is a very dangerous mental place to be and to please not fall into this trap. As I shared my experience with physically beating myself up, one of my friends in the corner laughed. Was she laughing because she didn't believe me or laughing at how shocked she was that I could open up that easily? Either way, I did not care. Whether or not I was in the middle of what nearly caused my life to end, I was always willing to try to help others diminish their distress.

For those of you who are familiar with eating disorders, you are likely well aware that the process of severely restricting food consequently tends to lead right into binge eating disorder. My story here is no different.

While every day was now filled with eating a Greek yogurt cup for breakfast and (usually) half of a quesadilla or tuna wrap for supper, it was only a matter of time before my body and mind "gave up." This is when the binging began to happen. If I had consumed even one cookie or any other edible treat, I became obsessed with the thought that I had given up. Even though the cookie was likely an extra 150 calories at most, I would think I had failed and would continue to eat everything in sight and anything I could think of—anything. At the beginning, I tried to vomit up my extra consumption but failed. I was terrified of throwing up so, oddly enough, that somehow saved me from having a struggle with bulimia as well. Instead, I began to punch my stomach. I was broken. I had tried so hard to be perfect for so long and now I had failed. I would continually punch my stomach to try to push it back in. I would shove my face in my pillow as I screamed profanities at the "failure" I had just committed. I would come back up for air and repeat this process. This lasted eight years.

The decade of my twenties is now remembered as a constant fight with binging and restricting. As you've previously read how my restriction took place, I'll bring you in sight with how the binging went. Another "perfect" day would be taking place; I would be eating far fewer calories than my recommended caloric intake, yet I would feel as if I was having a great day because I was "on track." By lunchtime, Hell broke loose. My cravings from so severely restricting became insane. I attempted to find a more-accurate synonym for insane, but insane takes the cake.

At first, I would simply give in to my deranged cravings. This may seem quite juvenile—cravings—but they quickly began to take over my entire life. Twelve o'clock would hit at work and I would nearly sprint to my vehicle and drive, as fast as possible, to McDonalds. At first, I would drive to any nearby fast-food restaurant to quite literally stuff my face with; however, McDonalds soon became an addiction. As I would pull-up to the drive-through window, I would order a supersized Big Mac meal complete with a Big Mac, large fries, large Coca-Cola, a wrap, an extra poutine and a Junior Chicken burger. A bit excessive, maybe? I could not help it. My cravings were so intense that **I HAD** to ensure I was ordering enough food to feel full. Ten minutes later and I had crammed every single last calorie down my throat. I now felt sick. The guilt, physical sickness and emotional anguish now set in. This took place nearly every single day until I was 28.

After a few years of alternating binging and restricting, I began to slowly gain weight. When I would hit a number over XXX pounds I would restrict myself as hard as possible, only to enter into another severe binge. I was now so filled with anxiety every single day from thinking I was "ugly" again that I would lose control.

This process of Hell took over every minute of every day. When I was successfully restricting, I was happy. The moment that my cravings took over or I gave into them, my life turned upside down. I would begin to shake. I would cry. I would run to the bathroom to hide in a stall pulling my hair to try to mask the emotional pain with something physical. I would sit at my desk at work and jab my high heel into my foot to try to shut my mind up. On a drive home I would cover my mouth and scream like I was dying because the emotional and physical pain were too much. One minute later, I would talk to my family on the phone or drive back to work and no one would know anything had transpired. This is how those who appear "strong" are in suicide-related news. Be kind to everyone; I was smiling through depression and no one knew.

Now, for those of you who have never struggled with binge eating, I need to make it clear that binge eating is far different from overeating. In my experience, while you are overeating you have a choice; you're aware that you're eating too much. Maybe it's just mom's home-cooked Thanksgiving meal, freshly baked cookies or a potluck with friends. I have overeaten on countless occasions and am now well aware of what the difference is between overeating and binge eating. When you are binge eating you lose control. You fight your mind until your mind takes over and you find yourself alone, hiding from everyone, in the corner of your pantry or the driver's seat of your car as you're parked in an abandoned parking lot of a closed school. You consume thousands of calories in mere minutes as your mind brings you to tears. The idea of stopping does not even cross your mind because the monster that you've just unleashed has complete control.

The National Eating Disorder Information Centre website states,

> Binge-eating disorder is characterized by recurring episodes of binge eating. It is important to note that overeating and binge-eating are not the same. Overeating can be described as consuming more food than your body needs at a given time. When a person overeats, it may be simply because the food is available and is very appetizing. An example of overeating may be eating a second serving of dessert after a full meal. Most people overeat on occasion. Binge-eating is much less common and is marked by psychological distress.

Although this is the clinical definition and not one's first-hand recollection of this disorder, it gives you a brief understanding of this disorder's underpinnings.

The NEDIC website further states the following,

1. A binge-eating episode is characterized by:
   a) The consumption of an unusually large amount of food during a relatively short period of time.
   b) Feeling out of control over what and how much is eaten and when to stop.
2. A binge-eating episode also includes three or more of the following:
   a) Eating very quickly.
   b) Eating regardless of hunger cues, even if one is already full.
   c) Eating until uncomfortably or painfully full.
   d) Eating alone due to embarrassment about the type and quantity of food ingested.
   e) Feelings of self-disgust, guilt, and depression.
3. The binge-eating episodes are not followed by compensating behaviours, such as in bulimia (excessive exercise, self-induced vomiting, or the misuse of laxatives or diuretics).

Binge-eating is seen as a disorder when the bingeing episodes occur at least once a week for three months or more.

Every single one of these descriptors are accurate. In my experience, they occurred numerous times per week for eight years.

This eventually hit the point where I recognized I needed help. Recognizing you need help is only one step in the process, however. Once you realize this fact, there is a whole other component: reaching out for it.

THE FIRST STEP

"YOU CAN NEVER CROSS THE OCEAN UNTIL YOU HAVE THE COURAGE TO LOSE SIGHT OF THE SHORE."
—CHRISTOPHER COLUMBUS

I had just binged. I had just consumed my McDonalds meal—that consisted of thousands of calories—within 10 minutes and was in emotional distress. This had been likely the one-hundredth time this occurred and I was tired. I was physically sick, I was disgusted in myself and I was parked just down the road from work—having to go back within the next 10 minutes. As I looked up the phone number to my family doctor, I was trembling. When the receptionist asks "What do you need to see the doctor for," what the fuck do I say? That I am a mid-twenties emotional mess with an eating disorder who has had the term "suicide" skim through her mind, which it never had before? Within a minute the question was asked, to which I simply replied "eating disorder." The first step was done.

Although that was the hardest thing I had done up to that point, I felt relieved. I was going to get help. I was going to put this eight-year trip to Hell to rest. That's when I learned that support for mental health needs to be far more prevalent than what is presently found. Upon entering the doctor's office, I was not seeking a sick note from work. I was not seeking a pat on the back. I was seeking help to not fucking hurt myself because of the eight-year-long, life-altering and debilitating fight that I was currently undertaking. Yet, I sat there with a smile as the doctor entered the room.

"What can I help you with today?" The question was asked again. This time, I poured my heart out. I was so desperate for help that I revealed everything. I revealed my severe restricting and binging routine, I let her know that I had been depressed for years—which, upon trying to get diagnosed for years, I never did get put in touch with the right person—and I, quite simply, asked for help. The first question she asked me drove a dagger through my heart. "Are you being too hard on yourself?" That nearly knocked the wind right out of me. My demeanor and appearance are both healthy. I know that I am seen as a strong, congenial person and am aware that my weight "seems" to be "healthy" because of nearly starving myself followed by subsequent binging. I simply replied with "probably."

Although it was a very quick appointment once I came to the realization that she was not taking my nearly life-taking disorder seriously, she offered to put me in contact with a registered psychologist and dietician. She advised that she would greatly assist with any depression issues and dietary needs. Although this isn't exactly what I was seeking, I thought that the psychology aspect of it may be of assistance. I was supposed to have received a phonecall from her by Christmas; that call never came. When you reach out for help once, that is a huge leap in itself. When you don't receive the help you need, continue to quite literally fight for your life and want to reach out again because you are failing with your fight, it's nearly impossible to pick up the phone. As such, I did not follow-up.

It was only a few months before I hit rock bottom once more. This time, I had poured my heart into emails. I was emailing registered psychologists, psychiatrists and counsellors just to receive help from anyone. I thought that by using my written communications skills to portray the debilitating fight I was undertaking, that they wouldn't misinterpret my strong in-person demeanor. One person replied. The reply was stating that I would be put on a six-month waiting list, if interested. I feel like that's the point where many people give up. I had sought out professional help to, quite frankly, not take away my life. Instead, I was not taken seriously and did not receive the help I was so desperately seeking. The positive part of this memoir comes in soon, I promise.

SOCIAL MEDIA MALIGNANCE

♥

"BEAUTY BEGINS THE MOMENT YOU DECIDE TO BE YOURSELF."
—COCO CHANEL

At 29 years of age, I have now been utilizing various social media channels for roughly 15 years. Although Instagram, Facebook and Twitter are what find themselves on my iPhone X that is sitting on the corner of my desk, their predecessors—such as MySpace and MSN Messenger—were commonly found throughout my adolescent years.

As you have previously read, much of my adolescence was spent enduring bullying. However, with today's societal advancement and the fact that social media is the new norm, my heart aches for those growing up in a world where malevolent individuals are able to hide behind their computer screens. Previously, any technologically laden spats that I was part of were conducted over MSN Messenger. However, those were person-to-person conversations online. With the growth of social media, any negative comments published on any pictures or posts are now made public to those who are allowed to view them, or those who have extraordinary searching capabilities. Now, don't get me wrong. I thoroughly believe that social media can be used for building relationships, exploring endless possibilities, and gathering motivation and inspiration. It is unfortunate, however, that it's now much easier for "keyboard warriors" to publicly attack their prey.

Social media is often, quite unknowingly, a very dangerous comparator to others' lives. In the midst of my battle with eating disorders, I often took to Instagram for a glimpse into others' battles. With the search of two specific hashtags—"#eatingdisorders" and "#bingeeating"—I was provided with millions and millions of quotations, reflections, stories and pictures. This is where I began to become engulfed with the endless stories from every corner of the globe. Upon reading one story and her correlating success, I began to wonder why it was taking me so long to beat this debilitating disorder. She went on to state that it is a complete mental game. Although I agree, at the time it made me question my ability to truly overcome my battle. A bit further down was another individual begging for help as she was close to committing suicide, and had various bruises and discolorations scattered across her body from malnutrition. Upon searching a bit further, it was dangerously easy to find fake "coaches" and individuals who were willing to "help you get your life back," without any comprehension, education or knowledge on the subject. It is extremely easy to create fake online accounts with the sole intention of publicly shaming others or attempting to make a quick dollar. Please, be cautious with your use of social media and be careful whom you trust.

Now, I must admit that over the past number of years I've become addicted to social media. Upon scrolling through millions of online profiles on one social media channel, it quickly became apparent how over-sexualized and unrealistic millions of posts are. Did I fall into this trend? Absolutely. For years throughout my twenties, I began to follow various beauty-filled and fitness-inspired social media accounts. Although by this point fitness and beauty were large parts of my life—and not in a negative sense—the wrath of needing to be seemingly perfect on the Internet took over.

Take a close look at some of the pictures you see on social media. Do you see bent bars? Is there seemingly perfect skin, right above where the skin appears to be that of a normal state? Do you see a body that seems a bit unrealistic? Can you even find kneecaps on the individual? This phenomenon of needing to appear perfect on social media has become the norm and, for quite a while, I fell into it.

Upon returning from one trip to Mexico a couple of years ago, I posted a picture of me in a bikini overlooking the pool from my bedroom balcony. Within a mere few minutes of posting the picture on social media, a comment quickly picked out that the bars I was leaning on appeared bent. At first, I was confused. I thought I had been so sneaky by altering my waist and hips to appear a tiny bit smaller, although by doing so I had unknowingly altered the appearance of the bars just ahead of me. Although it was an actual photographer who had picked out my dishonest alteration, these types of adjustments and edits are extensively found throughout millions of profiles. The edit also took me approximately 45 seconds to complete on a downloaded application from the iTunes Store. As I write this, I am disgusted in myself.

Unless one has been honest and publicly discloses that a photograph has been altered, there is no real way of determining if something has been edited. Why do we choose to do this to ourselves? Is it for a few extra "likes" on our picture? Give me a break. With the abundance of social media influencers, it's easy to see how people—myself included—become envious of others' lifestyles. However, we are only given one life to live. We must live **our own** lives to the fullest.

Another common trait found among various online profiles is the "perfect angle." Although this isn't what directly correlated with the commencement of my eating disorder, I can see this being a large trigger for young individuals today and in the future. Again, I must admit that I have been guilty of this as well. By posting a seemingly innocent picture of my sister and I having a fun time tanning in my backyard, I would be showcasing our congenial relationship, correct? Unfortunately, no. If you were to look a bit closer, you would see that my phone—which was somehow held awkwardly in my hand without falling out—was positioned high above the back of my head, allowing my hipbones to prominently show within the picture. I might have even added a little shadowing to ensure the depth between my hipbones to lower stomach was shown. As I quickly sucked in my stomach and held my breath, thus not allowing myself to breathe for a short period of time, I would capture the image. The picture was ready for social media.

Although social media can quickly become a very dangerous tool if used carelessly, it is also something that can connect varying cultures, languages, and corners of the world from a six-inch screen that you can grasp in the palm of your hand. When used correctly, social media can assist with building relationships; it can inspire a generation and reach those who are seemingly impossible to connect with. Social media can, and will, change the shape of the future.

I thoroughly believe that there is no harm in wanting to enhance one's self without going overboard. Whether you want to have your nails done, get your hair dyed or plump your lips, I have no problem with others wanting to feel better for themselves and themselves only. However, I'm tired of society trying to hide the realities that make us all beautiful. We are all beautiful and interesting in our own ways; that is what makes us each individual. The dangers of social media can be slowly diminished if we each consciously choose to reflect the realities of our own lives.

WHEN FIGHT BECOMES FOUGHT

♥

"THERE IS ONLY ONE WAY TO AVOID
CRITICISM: DO NOTHING, SAY NOTHING, AND
BE NOTHING."
—ARISTOTLE

Eleanor Roosevelt once stated "No one can make you feel inferior without your consent." This old adage has been a source of inspiration for many; however, I personally seem to struggle when attempting to connect with this quote. Do I struggle with this because Roosevelt was in a substantial position of power when she made this confidence-filled statement? Maybe. However, as you have now read, I have previously been made to feel inferior without my consent.

Although I unquestionably understand where Roosevelt was coming from—which seems to be the same place that modern-day bloggers gather all of their "fuck-the-haters" and "don't-care-what-anyone-thinks" mentalities—the truth is that words hurt. However, not only are you immediately proven to be better than those who attempted to put you down, but you're also able to overcome and grow from the unnecessary and uncalled for hatred that you feel. You are not weak. If we all feel alone in a single moment, we are all together.

It's now more apparent to me than ever that supports for mental health issues need to be far more prevalent than they are today. However, even if you aren't receiving the professional help you are seeking, you **ARE** able to overcome your fight, you **WILL** overcome it and people, such as I, **ARE** willing to listen. Never give up fighting and the term "fight" will become "fought."

As I write this chapter to my memoir, I can state with confidence that I have successfully beaten this debilitating disorder that is so prevalent in society today. Why is it so hard for society, as a whole, to openly discuss this mental and physical health issue that affects millions of Americans every minute of every single day? We need to become further educated. Doctors need to understand that just because someone "looks healthy," they are not "just being hard on themselves." Society needs to understand that if someone still appears to be overweight, they may have just lost 30 pounds and can out-run and out-lift the person who appears to be physically fit. Alternatively, society also needs to understand that the seemingly "physically fit" girl may have just thrown up her last meal. There needs to be more support, more advocacy and more empathy so that those who continue to struggle can know they are not alone. **You are not alone.**

"Education is the most powerful weapon which you can use to change the world" (Mandela, A). I find this quote to resonate very strongly with my individual fight as research is one component that assisted me in overcoming my disorder. As I wasn't receiving the professional help I had sought, I took to research to assist with my educational advancement on the subject. There are countless and countless memoires, "how-to" guides and blogs engulfing the Internet; however, as each fight is individual, you must find what resonates with you.

If you're worried about how much time it will take to overcome your disorder or reach a goal, the time will pass anyway. Continue to research, continue to educate yourself and be open-minded. At one point, I had even reached out to a well-known local fitness coach. With a background in psychology and advanced knowledge on eating disorders, she seemed to be the perfect fit **for me**. She fully understood and had worked with numerous individuals who also struggled and allowed me to message her anytime I felt a binge coming on. Find yourself a support system, even if just one person, and utilize it. There are people who can and are willing to help, and I promise you that you will overcome whatever is hurting you.

Coming out of high school with others' set perceptions of who I was and am was what lit the fire and ignited my passion for physical and mental health. I didn't write this memoir to receive empathy or to brag about what I've been through. I wanted to share my story because I am now in a very strong and empowered place in my life, and am willing to be an advocate and positive voice for those who struggle to be heard. If I were given the opportunity to go back and erase the pain I have been through, would I? Absolutely not. All of my past experiences have brought me to where I am today: an incredibly strong, intelligent and empathetic 29-year-old who is a passionate advocate for mental and physical health; a sister, daughter, friend and wife who is not afraid to stand up for what is right.

Be yourself. Do not be afraid to be the goofy computer nerd who sounds like a horse when she laughs; I'm clearly referring to myself. Do not give up what makes you feel beautiful, whether that's aesthetics or an escape to the ocean—my favourite place in the world. Do not allow yourself to be overtaken by assumptions. Do not judge a book by its cover, for—in my case—if you simply open the book to bypass the platinum blonde hair and heel clicks, you will find someone who is willing to reveal all of her insecurities and struggles, and someone who craves to help others realize their potential and achieve their goals. You'll find a trucker-mouthed, sarcastic, giggly girly girl with a tomboy attitude. You'll find a soul that was hurt badly in its adolescence, but one that has persevered and been called an "inspiration" by others. You'll find that your assumptions were completely inaccurate; this extends far past simply myself.

Teachers, please pay attention to the student who has no one to talk to during class. Don't disregard the student who often skips school, because they may truly want to be there but are scared to walk through the front doors. Please do not assume the silent ones do not want to be engaged; they may just be scared to speak out because the student next to them, and their 12 friends in the corner, are waiting for the next opportunity to publicly embarrass them. Please do not give up on your students.

Parents, I know it's hard. I am not yet a mother, but I know it's hard. If your child is acting out, it may be from the pain they are enduring on a daily basis. Pay attention to the time you spend with them when they're not feeling pressured by external factors; pay attention to the person whom you know they truly are. Continue to push them forward. Offer them a home where they feel safe from emotional and physical pain. Please do not give up on your children.

For anyone struggling, my heart aches for you. However, always remember that you are not alone. You are your own worst critic, you are beautiful and you are enough. The beginning of a journey starts with a single step. Please do not give up.

Allow yourself to make mistakes; they're part of what makes like interesting. Heck, they can even be fun. Whatever stage you're at in your life or whatever you're battling, it does get better. Never stop fighting and it will stop becoming a fight. I believe in you. We are all given one life to live; the only way to change tomorrow is by speaking up today.

EPILOGUE

"EVERY CHILD IS AN ARTIST. THE PROBLEM IS
HOW TO REMAIN AN ARTIST ONCE HE GROWS
UP."

—PABLO PICASSO

Through the corner of my eye, I just saw a text message from my husband flash across my iPhone X stating "My back hurts from Pumba." This is a daily occurrence for me, as attempting to roll a 50-pound English bulldog in the middle of the night is not a simple task. However, you would think it would be easy to fall asleep, given that—as anyone who has ever owned an English bulldog knows—their flatulence is enough to make anyone pass out.

Although we spent a pretty penny on purchasing our baby girl—the best purchase we have ever made—the message goes a bit deeper. I'm admittedly a "little shit," as my sister would so benevolently call me. Persistence, for myself, has proven to be a positive attribute through the past number of years. For as long as I can remember, I have always wanted an English bulldog. When I first moved to Saskatoon, I would always point down Attridge Drive stating I wanted to one day live "down there." Furthermore, I would find myself driving past one of the largest corporate buildings in Saskatoon whispering "I'm going to work there one day." Fast-forward to my present position and you'll find me leaving work at one of the most reputable organizations in Saskatchewan as I drive to my newly built home in Brighton—just down the road from Attridge Drive—with my English bulldog waiting as she snores on the couch.

"A river cuts through rock, not because of its power, but because of its persistence" (Watkins, J). As I just finished my third phonecall in the last two hours with my mother—this is nearly an everyday occurrence—she concluded by stating "You're like a bull in a China shop." While this would be true when referring to my unrelenting klutziness, she was referring to my innate ability to push for what I want. Life is simply too short to wait for opportunities to arise; you must pursue what you want beginning today.

Although I still find it hard to think of myself becoming a mother in the near future—whether or not it's because I am terrified of attempting to live up to the high standard that my mother has set—I find myself becoming instantly protective of my future children. I am protective of those children who are presently growing up in the modern world that I have previously described. Now, as I conclude my memoir, I am thinking about my younger self. I am remembering the girl who hid in bathroom stalls while crying during lunch hours to hide from her peers. I am remembering the girl who simply wanted a best friend, but instead was brought to a place where her sorrows were drowned in substance abuse. I am remembering the girl who—if she applied herself— was obtaining upwards of 90 percent in her classes and was a remarkably talented classical piano player. I am remembering the girl who was fortunate enough to have had her parents never once give up on her. If I were able to say something to her now, what would I say?

Keep on smiling, baby girl. I know it's exhausting. I know it hurts. However, do not let them see your pain. Do not allow them the pleasure of knowing they hurt you. Do not be afraid to be your weird self—people like it.

Do not be ashamed of your friends; the ones who choose you are whom you'll be close to for the rest of your life. Respect your family; they will soon become your best friends, although not soon enough. When you're scared or feeling alone, go to them. Do not hide in your sorrow; allow yourself freedom from your own mind.

Find things you love to do. Listen to your mother's advice; she is always right. Study hard because doing well in school makes things just a little bit easier. Believe in yourself and others will as well.

When things get tough, which they will, remember that you are not alone. There are always people who want to and are willing to support you. The people who are putting you through Hell are just as insecure as they make you feel.

You are beautiful. You are your own worst critic. Do not miss out on life because you want to weigh 10 pounds less. Do not be afraid to reach out for help and do not allow failure to scare you. The most beautiful scenery is often found at the top of the highest climb. Keep your head up because everything turns out alright.

As stated by the infamous Seth Godin, "What I'm saying is that one person—okay, what I really mean is you—has everything. Everything you need to build something far bigger than yourself. The people around you realize this, and they are ready to follow if you're ready to lead." I was able to write this memoir because I am a woman who has been fortunate enough to have had a constant support system. I was able to publish this memoir because I am no longer scared.

ACKNOWLEDGEMENTS

"FAMILY IS NOT AN IMPORTANT THING. IT'S
EVERYTHING."
—MICHAEL J. FOX

To my mom —
You'll never understand how much it means to me that you never gave up on me. You've shown me what true love is; you've shown me what it means to always be able to count on someone. Because of you I've learned how to be confident, empathetic and a woman who strives to be just one-quarter of the person you've proven yourself to be. You are the most amazing, beautiful, trustworthy, intelligent and selfless person I have ever met. Although this pains me to write, you've always been right. Always—all along and forever will be.

To my dad —

Your congenial personality and contagious laughter have shown me that being yourself is a trait that will continue to be admired. You've never been afraid to help me with whatever I've needed and you've shown me how to be a strong woman, both emotionally and physically.

To my husband, Kyle —

You have never, ever let me give up on myself. You've been with me through the entirety of my eating disorder, and through the ups and downs of an amazing nine years thus far. You've become my rock, my best friend and someone who I know will always believe in me, even when I've lost the ability to believe in myself. I'm so thankful that you've been blessed with the morals you have because I love you with all of my heart.

To my little sister, Heidi —

This is the toughest one to write and I'm finding myself choking up as I hit each key on the keyboard. You are my best friend. You've shown me that it's okay to be the weird, crazy girl I am and that people do love you when you're simply yourself. You've taught me to be brave; you've taught me to stand up for myself. You've taught me more than I could ever write in one paragraph. I oddly want to wrestle you to get out my aggression because all I want to write is another book on how much I love you. You're the one true friend I've ever had. You are such a caring, beautiful, intelligent and downright crazy person. You will forever and always be my 'lil sis.

CONTACT ALI

♥

Thank you so much for taking the time to read my memoir. I hope I was able to shine a light on some of the experiences faced by millions of individuals worldwide and provide a source of inspiration.

inquiry.fedrau@gmail.com
www.alifedrau.wordpress.com

92120611R00066

Made in the USA
Middletown, DE
05 October 2018